The Pi... ...inbow

Claire Walsh

Artwork

Original art by Kerry Burrow.
Find her on Instagram @the_non_citizen

Printed in the United Kingdom
First Printing, 2021

ISBN: Print (Soft Cover): 978-1-912677-91-7

Published by Purple Parrot Publishing

www.purpleparrotpublishing.co.uk

To Lottie and Ella

For being the best daughters
a dying man could wish for.

You put your lives on hold and helped him
have the death he wanted.

*You are incredibly brave and I am
honoured to be your mum.*

Introduction

"Never let the perfect be the enemy of the good"[1]

A wise man taught me that.

My life is not perfect; not by any stretch of the imagination. But has it been good? Good enough? Hell yeah! I have had, and am having, a mighty fine life!

Not the words you would expect to hear from someone who was widowed aged just 45. Not the words you would expect to hear from someone who had their heart ripped out of her world by cancer. *Cunting cancer*, as we call it in my family. Not the words you would expect to hear from someone who sat holding the hands of their husband, whispering words of love, comfort and permission. Permission to die, as he took his last breath. Not the words you would expect to hear from a mother, a mother who had to comfort her daughters when their beloved father was here no more.

I don't know why you are reading this, I don't know if you were attracted to the title, the cover, or, maybe like me, death and dying is your uninvited specialist subject. The mastermind round nobody wants to win. But when it comes a knocking at your door, you have a choice.

---

1.   *Simon Jones, via Kevin Courtney, originally attributed to Voltaire*

You could choose the "ignorance is bliss" approach. Grasp life with both hands and keep a firm grip, normality rules; banishing death. Death could live in the cupboard under the stairs. Opening the door, just a crack, on the occasional day, allowing the mess to come tumbling out, then trying hard to slam the door away and keep it hidden.

Or you embrace it. Open your arms; inhale it.

Acknowledge it is inevitable and the more you know about it, the more you try to understand it. The more you prepare for it, the easier it will be right?

Neither way is right. I chose the latter. But that doesn't make me right. Apart from that aching hole in your heart – that longing to have them back, that desire to hold them just one more time, that knowledge that you would do anything, yes anything if someone offered you the opportunity to bring them back to life – one of the worst things is the world, and his NOT widowed wife, having an opinion on you, your life, their death and your grief.

I strive not to be that judge. I'm not writing this to tell you how to do it. If I was, I would probably have called the book – "An Idiot's Guide to being a Widow" or "How to Grieve My Way". Instead, these are my thoughts, ramblings and musings on my experience of grief.

Reading helped me, during that phase of wanting to acknowledge and prepare for death. I read blogs, books, social media posts, anything I could about others who were, or had been, in a similar position.

6

It helped; I didn't feel so alone. I wasn't the only person in the world experiencing such devastation. I could cry. Cry at the recounts I was reading; cry for them and their pain rather than cry for me and my pain.

So, this collection of writing, this book, is my attempt to pay it back, or pay it forward. I hope it helps you, in some small way. I hope you get to see my perspective without having to feel my pain, but I doubt it, because death and grief are inevitable.

Let's talk about it; let's write about it; let's read about it.

Let's own it.

I am not the person I used to be

My name is Claire and I am not the person I used to be.

I used to be scared of my own shadow, I was crippled by an anxiety disorder which left me always waiting for a disaster. I imagined disasters and catastrophes on a daily basis. I lived in fear of fear itself. I lived fearful of the worst thing in the world happening. And then it did.

Now don't get me wrong, I was happy, I loved my life with my wonderful man, he was my rock, my world, my raison d' etre. Throughout my illness he, some counselling and medication meant that I mostly lived a happy and fulfilling life. A life tinged with, but not defined by, moments of madness, anxiety, worry and fear. Aside from some periods of agoraphobia and depression, I lived a life I loved and I loved that man.

And then, of all the fears I had ever imagined, the worst thing happened. *Cunting Cancer.* Bowel cancer to be precise. Suddenly I was looking real fear in the eyes, head on, eyes wide, but not like a rabbit in the headlights, more like a warrior going into battle. Now I hate all those battle analogies that there are around cancer, but I felt like a knight in shining armour ready to do battle for my man. I toughened up, my job was to look after him, instead of him looking after me.

So goodbye Claire the scaredy-cat and hello Claire the champion; Claire the brave; Claire the warrior. My first quest was to look after him hoping he would get better. When it became clear that wasn't going to happen, my ultimate quest was for him to have the best possible death at home surrounded by the people he loved.

I was brave, yet petrified.
I was strong, yet broken.
I was me, yet not me.

The worst thing I could imagine happened. It left me a stronger, wiser, braver person than I was before. I hate all that 'everything happens for a reason' nonsense, but I do know if you have been through the worst pain imaginable there is not much left to be scared of.

My name is Claire
but I am not the Claire I used to be.

Grief Brain
Does it really exist?

If you have faced a significant bereavement, you will probably be nodding right now.

Poor memory, confusion, disorientation, lack of concentration – maybe even delusions as your brain struggles to process the loss and tragedy you have experienced.

Since your loved one died you may have found yourself doubting your memory and even your sanity with a selection of events such as these:

- Standing in a room not knowing how you got there or why you are there. lack of concentration
- Wondering why the kettle hasn't boiled, only to find the kettle in the fridge and the milk on the side.
- Meeting an old friend – someone you have known for years, but you can't remember their name. You can remember their dog's name, but not theirs.
- Watching a film, engrossed one minute and then suddenly recalling a conversation from 10 years ago and forgetting the film until the credits are rolling and you have no idea what happened.
- Getting home from the supermarket, unpacking your bags, putting the desperately needed teabags away, only to find another 3 boxes on the shelf.

- Perhaps the cruellest, enjoying a book, a film, a party and thinking to yourself, "Wow, I can't wait to tell Martin about that... he's gonna love it..." And then you remember.
- Having to read the same words on a page over and over again because your brain isn't taking the information in; you just can't concentrate.
- Flitting from one task to another, getting nothing finished because you just can't stay focused.

Yep it exists, alright.

This book, has been written by someone who has grief brain (and menopause brain!). So, it's written in small accessible chunks. It's not a story told in chronological order. You can dip in and out of it and read it in bitesize pieces.

I hope you don't have grief brain, but if you do, I hope this style makes it easier for you.

Sorry, I can't help with the kettle in the fridge though!

Have You Walked in My Shoes?

Have you walked in my shoes?

Have you lost the man you shared your life with, the man you loved worshipped and adored?

Have you watched your daughters weep, in grief, at the loss of the best dad a girl could have?

No? Then don't judge me.

Have you nursed a man consumed by pain and losing his mind, whilst trying to preserve his dignity?

Have you crawled up the stairs, exhausted, silent tears rolling down your face, ready to paint on a smile and jump to action at the next emotional or physical demand?

No? Then don't judge me.

Have you felt the pain searing through your chest as you hold your lover's hand, whilst they take their last breath?

Have you stood brave in front of a crowded room and spoken a eulogy, when all you want to do is curl up and die?

No? Then don't judge me.

Just as I haven't lived your life, you haven't lived mine.

You think I am different – changed, and you are right.

I do not judge you and you have no right to judge me.

Some days my shoes are pink and sparkly, some days my shoes are dark and heavy.

Some days my feet will skip light-heartedly in my shoes, keen to explore and experience this wonderful world. Some days my feet will be heavy, dragging along with reluctance and resistance.

I will leave you to walk in your shoes.
Leave me to walk in mine.

When the Shit Hits the Fan

Sometimes death sneaks up on us. No warning; an instant, world shattering, unexpected, unwelcome, unwanted surprise.

> "Hello, I'm Death and I have just taken your person. My bad."

Sometimes death is more courteous and sends a nice polite warning, giving you time to adjust, prepare and get used to the impending,

> "Hello, I'm Death and I have just taken your person. My bad."

You have no choice over which you get. You might think you know which you would prefer but, truth is, it matters not. It is what it is and you will get on with whichever card you are dealt, in whatever way you can.

We got the,

> "Hello, I'm Death and I'm inviting myself to dinner; every dinner for the next 676 days."

Being over 60, my person Martin routinely received a shit kit through the post. Scoop a bit of poop. Pop it in the post. Wait a while for the results. He had done it before and there was no reason to think that August 2013 would be any different.

But it was different this time. The postie delivered a letter that said, 'Please redo this test as the results are inconclusive'. Martin said "Actually babe, I've not been feeling great. I do think there is something wrong."

It hadn't been the best summer holiday we'd ever had. Both being teachers, we usually made the most of the long six weeks' holiday but this year Martin had been more lethargic, sleepier and he was suffering from the most awful back pain.

So, he redid the bowel screening test but he also made an appointment with the doctor who fast tracked him, and boy was it fast. Our National Health Service at its best.

Within a week we were sitting in the bowel screening clinic in front of a very thorough and professional nurse called Charlotte.

She asked a series of questions, listened to Martin's answers and said, "I think we need to get you a Colonoscopy as soon as possible."

As soon as possible turned out to be the very next day.

We had been holidaying in our caravan, our little slice of heaven in the Lancashire countryside.

We returned to the lack of concentration caravan shocked at the speed, but impressed at how the NHS were taking things seriously and working at some speed!

After less than 24 hours of bowel preparation (use your imagination). We returned to the hospital for the colonoscopy. A huge hug before he went down a long corridor, leaving me leaky eyed and anxious. I sat in the waiting room for the long wait. The nurses told me he'd be gone for about an hour. So, I pulled a trashy novel from my bag and started to read.

I don't recall how much I read.

I don't recall if there was anyone else in the waiting room.

I don't recall much really.

But I do recall the nurse was back by my side in about 10 minutes.

"Mrs Walsh, the doctor wants to speak to you and Mr Walsh."

Her face said it all.

She looked at me with pity.

My stomach dropped and I was fighting back tears as I followed her down the corridor to a room where Martin sat, alone. She left us and we held hands, speechless, whilst waiting for the doctor to appear.

I've always thought doctors and nurses were admirable people. It takes some guts to do what they do – especially when they have to tell people the worst news.

Only he didn't really tell us. He asked Martin if he had any idea why they had ended the procedure so quickly. Martin replied, "I think I have cancer and I think the camera got as far as the tumour and couldn't get any further."

The doctor nodded. "You're right – I can't officially 100% say it's cancer until the results from the biopsy come back, but having seen the tumour, I'm sure that you have cancer."

Ever the gentleman, Martin held out his hand and shook the doctor's. "Thank you, Dr. Thank you for your honesty."

I, of course, burst into tears, those silent tears that roll down your face without stopping, as if your eyes have developed a leak. Martin didn't cry. He stayed calm and quiet as the doctor explained the practicalities of what would happen next.

Those of you who have experienced something similar may understand the conflicting feelings I had at the time.

It felt so real; yet not real at all.

It felt unexpected; yet as if it was always going to happen.

It felt unbearable; yet I knew I had it to bear.

It felt heartbreaking; yet I knew I couldn't indulge that heartbreak.

I get really fed up with the battle language used around cancer but if I'm honest, at that stage that was what was in my mind... I couldn't indulge that sadness, that heartache,.

There was a fight to be had and together Martin and I would win.

Of course, I'm now a widow. So does that mean we didn't win? Hell no. We are all going to die and cheating death is impossible. Winning is about what you do with your life and my wonderful husband lived it to the full and loved those around him, truly, madly, deeply, fully until he took his last breath.

Don't count the days, Make the days count

And in my mind that makes him a winner.

Another "Happy New Year" without you.

Dear Martin,

It's January 2017 and you ceased to exist in June 2015 so I'm now on my second "new year" without you.

I still don't believe in an afterlife, heaven or any such thing. I wish I did, then maybe I could be comforted by thoughts that you were watching me, guiding me and supporting me. You would know how many of your predictions came true.

So I feel compelled to write to you. A letter you will never read, because you are dead.

After 23 years together, just 2 without you feels such a minuscule amount. Yet it also feels like a lifetime.

Things I wish you knew:

I wish you knew that I was happy. You told me so many times that I would be, but I argued back. How could I ever be happy without you? It was impossible- but guess what? I am. It's a different

sort of happiness. A happiness tinged with sadness - how crazy is that? It's the happiness of someone who has had their world turned upside down. The happiness of someone whose heart has been broken. However, that means I appreciate every moment even more because I know everything can change in the blink of an eye.

I wish you knew that our gorgeous daughters have shown such courage and determination. They are both living their lives and showing such bravery as they keep on moving forward, refusing to give up because they want to make you proud. And my word, you would be proud!

I wish you knew, that as predicted, not everyone handles change so well and some relationships may not survive your death and our grief. Sad but true. You shared with me your own experiences of life after loss and how this had happened to you. I try to keep your positive open arms approach but sometimes this is a challenge. But hey, I've faced worse.

I wish you knew I have a new job and have conquered so many of my own phobias and mental health issues! My mantra since you died is "I'm strong, I'm brave and I can do anything." I didn't believe it at first but yet again, as you predicted - if you fake it, eventually you feel it!

I wish you knew I have a new relationship and I've been brave enough to love again even though that means I may face loss again. I remember you giving the girls a talking to before you died and saying, "When your mum

gets a new partner
you must be nice to
them. She is too young
and too much fun to
be a lonely old widow"
Thank you. I'm pleased
to report that they are
lovely to him and refer to
him as NBT (the next best
thing)! He's not you but
he's the next best thing!
Which coming from them
is a compliment indeed!

Most of all, I wish you knew that
you have not been forgotten. We
all talk about you all the time
and speak your name so
often, remembering
the amazing man
you were. Our lovely
granddaughter
remembers you even
though she was so young.
She watches videos of you
and her together and has
such precious memories of
you.

Thank you for our wonderful life together.
I would ask you to write back soon but we
all know that's not going to happen.

I love you.

Till death do us part doesn't quite cut it
because the reality is, love doesn't end
with death.

Because somethings are
outside time.

Love always

Claire x

You Think!

You think you know what being a widow is
because your dog died.

You don't.

You think it's ok to pretend he didn't exist,
for fear of reminding me.

It's not.

You think it's time I got over it,
it's been six years after all.

Never.

You think it's ok to tell me
he wouldn't want me to cry.

Duh!

You think it's ok to tell me
he's in a better place.

No.

Nowhere is better than in my arms.

You think you can't be happy if you are sad.

You can.

You think to love another stops the love for him.

It doesn't.

You think that your sympathy makes me feel better.

Nope.

You think I should be grateful for your pity.

I'm not.

You think I am different.

I am.

I Remember

I remember the day we were told that Martin had days, possibly weeks but certainly not months to live. I remember the day so well. It was February 2015.

If I close my eyes and think of it, I can still feel the pain, I can still taste the bitter disappointment of the inevitable. I can still see the bleak prospects of a life without him. What I didn't know then was that they were wrong, not about the inevitable but about the timescale.

We would have months!

That crazy, stubborn, determined, wonderful man didn't die until June!!! There were amazing moments, there were scary moments, there were hard moments and there were beautiful moments.

Most of all there was life, LIFE!

I know that Martin treasured his life and was determined to enjoy whatever was left of it, in whatever way he could. Watching someone living and dying at the same time changes you. We are all different but for me it has made me more determined to live my life well. I have what he was denied so I have a duty to live life to its max.

I am still here for a reason.

Of course, I've had the duvet days where the grief is too great and winds its way around my body like a boa constrictor, squeezing the life out of me, incapacitating me so that all I can do is stay in bed and cry. When I have those days I indulge myself and give myself permission to be sad, miserable and devastated for as long as I need.

But on most days I feel the best tribute I can pay to Martin is to live my life with purpose, packing it full with crazy fun, love and laughter.

If you can, if it's possible for you today, grasp life with both hands and do something fun. Enjoy every moment possible and appreciate the tiniest moments of joy.

If it's not possible, if today is a tough day for you, accept your sadness, embrace your grief, cry, scream, shout and hate the world if you need to. Surround yourself with people who won't judge. When you are ready, return to a positive place and remember, life is precious. You are still alive and try your hardest to make your life a tribute to them.

#lifeispreciousliveitwell
#stillhereforareason

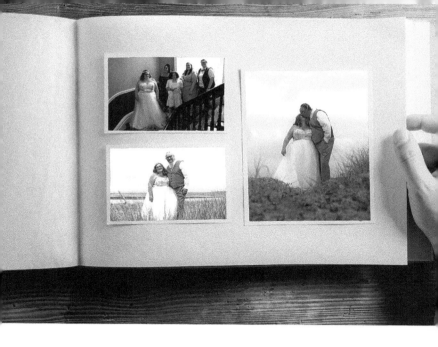

To Love and Love again

To say I never think of the man that
came before is untrue.

Once you love someone they stay in your heart forever.
Love never dies.

To say loving the man that came after is betraying the
man that came before is untrue.

I spend every day living life to the fullest in tribute
to Martin – the man who came before – whilst loving
Simon – the man who came after. The man who helped
me carry on writing my story.

Happily Ever After

One evening as I read my six-year-old granddaughter a story, we said those famous last words and I asked her the question "What does happily ever after mean?"

She replied "Like you and Grandad. You lived happily ever after – until he died."

I felt a moment of sadness, tears threatening to leave my eyes but I took a deep breath. She wasn't finished yet. "Now you live happily ever after with Simon. Until he dies, or you do!"

Any sadness I felt disappeared, replaced with pride. Six years old and she got it! No sadness in her voice, no grief in her eyes. Just matter of fact. A six-year-old with an immense understanding of life and death. We are all here to live our lives as happy as we can and then we will die!

Martin had a wonderful death at home surrounded by the people he loved. That included children. Some may have frowned at our openness and honesty with them. After all we have an inherent desire to protect our children from pain and hurt. To shield them from death for fear of making them sad or scared.

The children in Martin's life were offered no such shield. Grandchildren, nieces and nephews were told with honesty, at their own level of understanding, that he was dying, and that once he was dead, they would never see him again. All that would be left were memories.

So what was really important was
to make memories and share happy times.

So, that's what we did, be it riding up and down on the hospital bed which became a feature of our lounge, a science experiment, watching the football, eating cake or joining him in watching his final sunset at the beach. We made memories.

I believe that honesty, openness and focus on good memories is what has helped my beautiful granddaughter be so resilient, so strong and so comfortable with life and death. If you ask her where her grandad is she would answer clearly,

"He's in my head and my heart."

He may be dead, but he lives on in our heads through our memories and in our hearts through the love we have for each other.

Despite my loss I am lucky because, hand on heart, I can say "and they lived happily ever after".

I hope you are living your lives well and are writing your own happy endings. I know some days are tough and happily ever after seems like a distant memory or even a futuristic dream; but if you can, try to fake a little smile and live life as if it's a fairy tale... a twisted fucked up fairy tale, where the evil stepmother is death and the pea under mattresses is a lump in your throat so big you can hardly breathe but a fairy tale none-the-less and remember to live... happily ever after.

Happy Death Day

We celebrate and commemorate life's significant events birthdays, anniversaries and even divorces. But how do we mark the actual day of a loved one's death? I've struggled with this throughout my grief journey I must confess.

I'm often not great on the run up to the day – the anniversary... *the deathiversary* . I love my happy memories and rejoicing in the great times we had during our 23 years together.

But I do not love the memories of our last few weeks together.

There was still some laughter, there was plenty of love but I'll be honest, for the most part, the last 48 hours were hell on earth.

Martin wanted to die at home with no strangers involved and as little medical intervention as possible. I am immensely proud to say that we managed that. I couldn't have done it without my gorgeous girls, who also always have the prospect of Father's Day without him so close to the anniversary of his death.

I wish I could ease their pain.

Team Martin rocked. Whether you were part of the inner trilogy caring for the man we loved, whether you were one of the daily or weekly visitors raising spirits, having a laugh, doing mundane jobs like taking the bins out or whether you were one of those who could no longer face coming and watching him die but still sent texts or called with messages of love and support – whoever you were, whatever you did, we can be proud he got the death he wanted.

And I don't regret it for a single moment...

Each year, the run up to D-Day – death day – sees me reliving the trauma of watching that wonderful man die and it makes me sad. It makes my heart hurt just like it did on day one. It makes tears never be far from my eyes. It makes me snappy and resentful towards people moaning about trivia.

In a strange way, I end up looking forward to the anniversary of the day he died.

The day he stopped feeling pain.
The day he found release from the torture
of those last few days.

So on those days I say *"Happy Death Day"* to the man I love and get on with remembering our wonderful life together. I carry on living my life to the fullest because I am lucky to be alive, I am lucky to have two beautiful daughters. I am lucky to have family and friends. But most of all,

*I am lucky to have had such love in my life
and to still be alive to have the opportunity
to carry on loving others.*

So I try, when I can, to mark and remember Martin's life
in the way he lived, the way he died,
with love and happiness.

Imagine a World

Imagine a world that is both upside down and inside out. Where you once enjoyed living, but now you don't. It used to be a happy place filled with love. Now it is a sad place filled with grief; love with nowhere to go.

Imagine a world that was full of light, laughter, twinkling eyes and smiles aplenty. A lush landscape of love. Rich and fertile, where love grows and multiplies like a field of dandelions. Now its dry, arid soil only supports an ecosystem of pain and misery.

Imagine a world filled with joy, where your heart skips a beat when you see your lover. Now your heart feels pain instead of joy. Real pain, physical pain like a cramp in your heart with no way to ease it. If you've felt it, you will know what I mean, broken hearted doesn't even begin to cover it.

Imagine a world where your truth was love but now there is no truth. Now life is a lie, a big fat fucking lie. You smile and pretend because life goes on. If you are lucky you can fake it till you make it and the lie becomes the truth. You may even have moments of new love and happiness, if you are lucky.

Imagine a world where you might be brave enough to love again. The landscape watered by hope and trust so love may be able to grow again, but fear grips you. The fear of losing love again mingled with the possibility of loving again.

Imagine that world. That is the world where us widows live.

When Tragedy Strikes

When tragedy strikes and death comes calling,
people are everywhere.

'I'm so sorry, how can I help?
I want you to know that I care.'

When tragedy strikes and your love is gone,
people are caring and kind.

'What do you need? Don't be lonely.
Call anytime, you know I don't mind.'

When tragedy strikes and grief is constant,
support starts to fade away.

No phone calls, less texts, friends start to say,
'Sorry I'm busy today.'

When tragedy's past and you don't 'get over it'
you are considered a bore.

They don't want to listen, they stop
including you.
Just when you needed them more.

The day my world turned upside down

29th August 2013. The day we sat in a small room waiting for the doctor who had just had a camera up Martin's arse!

The procedure had been too quick. They had to stop early. The doctor asked Martin why he thought they had stopped.

Martin said because I have cancer and you couldn't get past the tumour. The doctor agreed.

These are all facts. It is easier to remember facts than feelings. The feelings are too hard to describe.

Sadness, so deep, sadder than you have ever felt in your life, silent tears falling from your eyes in a perpetual stream of sadness. You are aware of them, soaking your face yet you can't stop them, you can't even wipe them, you just let them roll.

Fear, so paralysing, you can't speak, you feel sick, your stomach is flipping. Your mouth is watering, you feel that you may vomit, right there on the doctor's shoes, uncontrollable fear, more scared than you have ever been in your life.

Even these memories of those feelings are not as intense as the actual feelings. Time makes us forget them, like childbirth we think we can remember it but our brains cleverly water down those feelings. Because if we felt them as they truly were for longer than was necessary, we would not be able to live, we would not be able to breathe, we would not be able to move forward.

And we must move forward. The best tribute we can make to those who have died is to live our lives with love, with hope, with happiness. If only it was that easy though.

Grief is not linear, grief is not straightforward, grief is not the same for everyone. One day can be good, the next day can be awful. But having experienced such a loss, having experienced such grief I am changed.

I appreciate life more.

I don't sweat the small stuff so much.

I love deeply, even though this scares me.

I am grateful for everyday I open my eyes.

I forgive more.

I crave experiences not things.

Little things make me happy.

I am less tolerant of those who waste
their time being angry.

I am brave and I take risks.

I feel more empathy with the pain of others.

I get frustrated with people who cannot see
the beauty before their eyes.

I encourage others to be positive.

I enjoy the pleasure of others as much,
if not more, than my own.

I wish others could have my perspective,
but not my pain.

Martin Walsh will always be my happiest memory
and my saddest memory.

29th August 2013 — the day my world
turned upside down and I am changed.

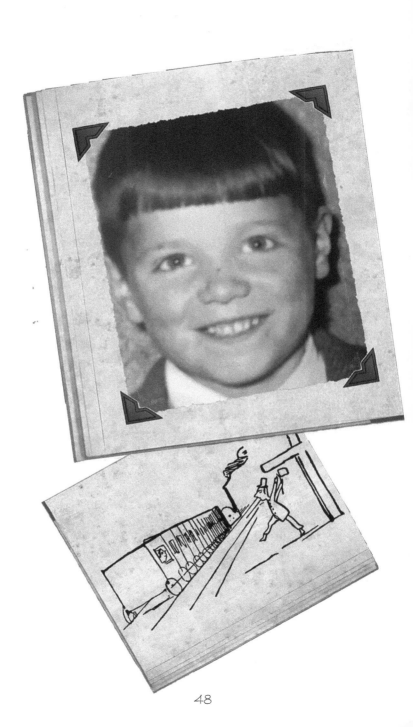

The In-Between.

I did some filing. Sorting paper and "stuff" that has just been in a pile at the top of my wardrobe.

Amongst that "stuff" was a maroon-coloured file. I knew it was there but I had avoided opening it, for more than two years.

Tasteful, sombre, serious. Strange words to describe a file but it is the file given to me by the funeral directors when that gorgeous man died. And stored in it, for two years are two defining certificates.

This week I was ready to hold those pieces of paper in my hands. One small square of old paper. Dated in November 1948. Telling the happy story of the birth of a baby boy named Martin Walsh. The other a larger A4 sized piece of paper, newer, fresher, crisper dated June 2015. Recording the sad story of the death of a man called Martin Walsh.

Life defined by two certificates.

Life defined by a start date.

Life defined by an end date.

Life beginning. Life ending.

Life defined.

Or is it?

Life is not about the beginning or the end. Life is about the in-between.

Some pieces of paper contribute to the story of the in-between. Wedding certificates, birth certificates of children. Love letters, cards, tickets, photos, the memorabilia you collect through life. Wondering why you keep it but being glad that you did.

But the record of the in-between is in our head and our hearts. The memories of our lives and the feelings we have. The in-between is good. The in-between is now. The in-between is life.

If you are reading this now. You are alive. You are living the in-between. You might be happy. You might be sad but you are writing your own in-between. Try, if you can, to make it a good story. Live in the now and enjoy life.

You already have the certificate that defines the start of your life. You don't know when your loved ones will get the certificate that defines the end of your life. So, enjoy the in-between because someday your story will live on in the head and the heart of others. And, as the late great Martin Walsh said,

"Life is for the living."

Where do you want to die?

We are all one day nearer to our death than we were yesterday. Yet rarely do we talk about it, acknowledge it, let alone plan for it.

Martin made a plan. A plan to have a good death, at home, with the people he loved.

Some people might think this sounds strange; your home is meant to be a special happy place, full of fun and love. But from the moment Martin was diagnosed with bowel cancer in 2013, he knew that it was the only place he wanted to be.

We were lucky because our local hospice, Trinity, had a Hospice at Home team. They helped that plan come to fruition.

They enabled me and my daughters, Lottie and Ella to give Martin a final act of love. I was aware of hospices, but I didn't know about all of the things they did. To be honest, I thought it was just a place you went to die. But when Martin's cancer was diagnosed as terminal, we were determined to be active and get on with everyday life. Trinity's team were like a 'security net' – they were always there if we needed them, always on the end of the phone.

Then in February 2015, Martin was so poorly he ended up in the hospital. I know how special the NHS is, but the hospital just wasn't the place for Martin.

*He wanted to be at home,
with his family and friends.*

They told us we didn't have much time left – just days. But Martin didn't like doing what he was told; we had another four months together.

It was so important for our family to care for Martin ourselves, as much as we could manage. This was one of the most important gifts that Hospice at Home gave us – the nurses empowered us to help, while still being there for the things we just couldn't do. I remember when Martin got a syringe driver, it would fall out all the time. But it was never too much trouble for the team to come out and fix it. Martin's eyes would light up when the nurses arrived because they weren't strangers – they were his new friends.

It sounds odd to say Martin's death was full of fun and love – but we laughed up until the very last day. One night, when we were all trying to sleep, Martin simply wasn't having it. Around 4 am, he started singing *'All You Need is Love'*. I tried to remind him how late it was, but in the end the whole house got up and sat round his bed and had a party. Without Hospice at Home, we simply wouldn't have had that time, together, in the place we spent our lives.

The night he died, Martin was with the people he loved – exactly where he wanted to be. Without the expert nurses at Trinity, I would have struggled. When I look back on it now, I think, what a wonderful thing it was. I know that we did everything we could have done. Because of that, we've been better able to cope with the grief and can look back on it with peace.

Martin had a good life and a good death.

I shall be eternally grateful that we had the power, the strength and the confidence to grant Martin his last wish.

Last Night I dreamt of You

I wandered through an unknown house,
looking for you my love,
I looked in every single room,
searching the attic above.

I asked every person that I met,
"Have you seen my Man?"
They shook their heads and answered ,"No".
I cried as only a widow can.

Like Groundhog Day I searched again,
around and round I went.
Alone trapped in my frantic search,
exhausted, on the wall I lent.

Shoulders hunched and head down,
my voice exploded into a scream.
Don't worry Claire, just wake up,
you know it's just a dream.

A bad dream, that's all it is,
I rouse myself from my sleep.
I wake up, remember you're dead,
and for real, I start to weep.

Kindness

Kindness is a gentle hug on the days
when things are tough.
A soft caress, acknowledging
they know you've had enough.

Kindness is a daily text,
to check how things have been.
Calling round, mop in hand,
announcing 'I'm here to clean',

Kindness is a gift in the post,
something to brighten your day.
Taking your mind off the diagnosis,
and the inevitable decay.

Kindness is a Marie Curie nurse,
offering a night of sleep.
Exhausted, you can climb the stairs,
crawl into bed and weep.

Kindness is still coming to visit,
even when it's tough to see.
Being there, for both of us,
caring for him and me.

Kindness is driving 370 miles
to be with a dying man.
Holding me, while I weep in your arms,
like only a parent can.

Kindness is the bad taste jokes,
and laughing till we cry.
Just accepting, it is what it is,
not asking the question why.

Kindness is the hospice at home,
coming night after night,
Not strangers, new friends,
doing all that is right.

Kindness is the moment of death
when all your pain has gone.
For me the pain is present still,
and forever will go on.

Christmas

There's something about 'The most magical time of year'. I'm sure if you ask most of us in the 'Widow Club' we would say that Christmas is tough.

But actually, the truth is every day is tough and Christmas is no different.

Except Christmas is full of expectations:

 The expectation that you will be happy – well guess what... it is sometimes difficult to feel happiness when you have watched your lover die.

 The expectation that you will celebrate – hmmmmm a tough one, I love a good party, but so did Martin and we partied right up to his death, and if I'm honest every party without him feels as if there's something missing.

 The expectation that dreams will come true, we will get our hearts desire and that the things under the wrapping paper will make us happy - the things that I desire cannot be wrapped, my dreams will not come true.

 The expectation that you will spend Christmas with the people you love – tough call when the person you love is dead.

Christmas is full of expectations and expectations can be dangerous. We make mental movies and imagine what the perfect Christmas looks like. We imagine what a perfect life looks like.

A wise man, the man who came after, has taught me not to let the perfect be the enemy of the good. I live in the now and enjoy the present rather than unwrapping presents.

So to get through Christmases I have made myself some Christmas promises:

 I will not let myself be ruled by expectations.

 I will accept my sadness and yearning for the past when it occurs.

 I will enjoy my happiness and contentment with the present when it occurs.

 I will enjoy all that is good and not desire the perfect.

I hope that you can too.
Free yourself from expectations.

Live in the now and never let the perfect be the enemy of the good.

New Year's Eve

New Year's Eve, a time for reflection, a time to celebrate the past and dream of the future. Old Year's Night, a time to remember, a time to reminisce and dream of new beginnings.

New Year's Eve gets us thinking about time, what has gone before, what is yet to come.

Time. It's a great healer, I hear! I miss him like he has been gone forever at the same time I love him as if he were here only yesterday.

Time, that precious commodity that runs out for us all in the end. I never used to wear a watch and would frequently ask "What's time babe"? He would answer, "It's the artificial unit of measurement of the passing of our lives". Ever the joker, I never tired of his jokes.

I have now had plenty of those artificial measurements of the passing of our lives without him. I've had sad days, bad days, good days and fucking

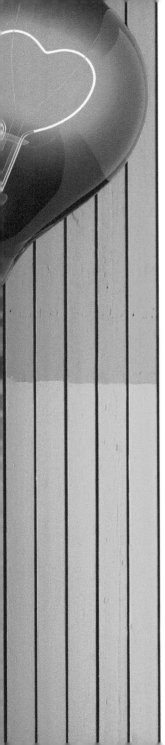

amazing days. Some days the pain is so much I do not think I can bear it, sometimes the joy is so much I do not think I can contain it.

But for each of those artificial units of measurements I have been alive. I wish he still was but I know I can't have that. So, I choose to celebrate his life by living mine. Enjoying those artificial units of the passing of my life whenever I can. No apologies. No regrets.

New Year's Eve:

 a time for remembering the great things that came before.

 a time of dreaming of the great things that are to come.

But most of all New Year's Eve, a time to enjoy the present, the here, the now, the artificial measurement of the passing of life.

21+3

Today is my 24th wedding anniversary. I was lucky enough to spend 21 of those years with my husband enjoying life and loving each other every day. We never went to sleep on an argument. We said "I love you" many times every day. We laughed together, we cried together, we lived together, sharing every detail of our lives.

But life can be a bitch and cancer is definitely a cunt! For the last three years I have had no choice but to live without him. And so I do! I still laugh, I still cry, I live my life with passion, determination and courage. Life is precious and I am lucky to be alive.

That positive attitude doesn't mean I don't have bad days. It doesn't mean I expect all widows to grieve the same. One thing I have learnt is that we all find our own ways of coping and mine is to be positive and love my new life.

Don't let anyone tell you how to grieve.
Don't let anyone tell you how to love.

 Memories

I wish I could remember every good night kiss. But memory doesn't work like that.

I wish I could forget death juice. But memory doesn't work like that.

So many memories that I love to recall.

So many memories that I would give anything to erase.

I remember the first time I saw you. I can recall the twinkle of your eyes, and the way my heart fluttered and tummy flipped as we talked for the first time.

I remember the last time I saw you; I held your hand and told you I loved you, as you took your last breath. Pain so immense in my chest. Who knew a broken heart hurt so much. I have never felt such pain... and I gave birth to a 10lb 6oz baby!!!

Six years on and I no longer trust my memory. Is it the menopause or is it grief? I don't know but I've lost count of the times I've forgotten where I am and what I'm doing. And don't even get me started on finding the kettle in the fridge!

So They Say

It gets easier, they say.

           Time is a great healer, they say.

You'll get back to normal, they say.

           The first year is the worst, they say.

You will get over it, they say.

           You will find closure, they say.

I'm not sure who they are, or why they say those things, because none of them are true.

If time is a great healer, why am I not healed? Why do I still have a pain in my chest and a broken heart, when I recall those last few days of his life and remember the sheer agony I felt when he took his last breath?

Time has passed since my world turned upside down. All our plans, mental movies of our future, our retirement, our life together as we grew old and wrinkly! Gone. Finished. Dead. How can I get back to normal? That was my normal and I cannot have it anymore. I now have to live with a new normal, a normal where he does not exist.

It's been years since that tenacious husband of mine decided it was time to let go of his firm grip on life and let his cancer ravaged body rest in peace. If the first year is the worst, then why do I find myself missing him more as significant events happen and he is not present. Or even the insignificant events – I finished a great book the other day and my first thought was, "Wow, I can't wait for Mart to read this – he is gonna love it". And then I remembered – he doesn't read anymore, he's not here anymore.

I have faced the biggest adversity of my life. I am resilient. I can face the future. I am strong, smart and brave but I will never get over it. I will never believe that "Life never gives you more than you can handle", because as strong as I am, there have been so many moments where I have cried myself to sleep and hoped that I didn't wake up in the morning. Life certainly gave me more than I should have to handle.

It has been years since that wonderful man died. Maybe that means he found closure but I have not and more to the point, I don't want to.

I want my memories, my love, my life to stay well and truly open. Grief is the price we pay for love and I am so lucky to have experienced that love, I wish I didn't have to feel this loss. But it's a price I'm willing to pay.

I will live my life with my loss, my grief and my pain. I will do it my way and not their way – because they don't know what they are talking about.

If you are grieving, do it your way, not their way.

If you are not grieving, lucky you. Don't judge those of us who are. Don't be one of "them". Have an open heart and be grateful that you do not have to live with our pain or our perspective.

Live and let live, or so they say!

The Crazy Widow

Those people who know me well know that I'm not only a widow but I'm a crazy widow. Long before I became a widow I suffered with my mental health and was diagnosed with a panic disorder and agoraphobia.

That illness shaped who I was and what I did for about 20 years. I found ways to cope and managed to live a good life, mostly, but that life was very much framed by my illness. At worst, I didn't leave the safety and security of my home at all. At best, I left my home only to go to the very few places I felt safe – work being one of them! I missed out on so much, but I consoled myself with the idea that, mostly, I could control my illness, rather than the illness control me. Who was I kidding?

I lived with daily irrational fears, crazy catastrophes and ever present imagined dangers.

Sometimes I managed to quell the craziness, sometimes not. Those fears would limit what I was able to do, where I was able to go.

I felt lucky to have family and friends, who accepted my madness and loved me all the same. Even when my phobias around travel meant that I couldn't go to visit them and they always had to put in the travel time to see me.

So, 20 odd years of being scared of the worst thing in the world happening and then it did... Martin was diagnosed with terminal cancer. Surely, I was going to go to pieces. Shockingly, I found that when something so awful, so scary and so devastating happens, there is no space for anxiety anymore, there is no need to catastrophise because you are already smack bang in the middle of your worst nightmare.

I put all of my energy into enjoying the time we had left. I put all of my efforts into looking after him and helping him have the positive death in the place he wanted with the people he loved. And even if I say so myself, I did a great job and I will be forever proud.

So bizarrely, although I have grieved greatly since he died, my mental health in these past few years has been better than it's been in a long while. You can have a mental illness but still have a good level of wellbeing. You can also grieve and still have a good level of wellbeing.

Of course, I still have days where my emotional wellbeing takes a tumble, the panic and anxiety creeps back in. It can get the better of me and take control. If I can, I think about Martin and what I had been through. I remind myself how brave I am, how loved I am and that my success rate for surviving tough days is 100%.

Christmas and Cancer

It's hard for me to think about Christmas without thinking about Cancer. The two are inextricably linked in my mind.

When I think about it, I believe it started around Christmas 2012. Moving furniture, a heavy sofa, Martin complained his back hurt. Not like him at all. A stereotypical bloke, who rarely complained and never went to the doctors.

In the new year, the pain was so bad that he went to the doctors. A pulled muscle they suggested. He carried on like a good bloke would.

It didn't get better though. He lost his appetite and started picking at his food. I threatened to divorce him if he didn't start eating properly – I love cooking and eating out and it offended me to see him pushing food around his plate. He later confessed to finding ways to hide food and avoid mealtimes, as if he had an eating disorder.

Christmas 2013 was going to be a good one. We had booked luxury lodges with hot tubs. Well planned, a truly magical Christmas, four generations of family, celebrating in style. What we hadn't planned for was the unwelcome guest. Cancer.

In August 2013 Martin was diagnosed with bowel cancer, so Christmas 2013 was our first Christmas with the knowledge that a tumour was present. The hidden guest from 2012 was well and truly making its presence known.

I'll spare you the gory details but by Christmas Eve he was so poorly, emergency surgery to put a stent through the tumour meant we spent our first Christmas Eve apart in 20 years. Him in Blackpool Vic, and me at Ribby Hall. Despite the love and support of my family, including some crazy cooking as they tried to replicate my recipes, I cried myself to sleep, and made two wishes. One that he would be able to come out of hospital in the morning and the other that cancer would fuck right off and he would be cured. Wishes do come true and he was able to come out of hospital on Christmas morning. If I could swap my 50% success option I'd love the latter wish to be the one that came true.

Christmas 2014, we knew it would be his last. The terminal diagnosis had been given in February 2014. Three-six months they said. So, Christmas 14 was a bonus, something to celebrate and so we did. It was my saddest and my happiest Christmas, we spent it at home surrounded by love, drenched in oxytocin, as we all knew there would never be a Christmas like it again.

And there wasn't.

Every Christmas since has been spent as a widow.

Some people describe those who die from cancer as losers, they lost their brave fight and all those battle metaphors.

Martin Walsh was no loser, and neither am I.

Cunting cancer will always be part of my Christmas but I refuse to let it win.

 Every happy memory, every sad memory. They are precious. *I win.*

 Every happy moment, every sad moment. They are precious. *I win.*

I'm not going to pretend I don't miss him at Christmas. I'm not going to pretend I've not cried at Christmas. Likewise, I'm not going to pretend I haven't been happy – I'm not going to pretend I've not had fun. Cancer you will not spoil Christmas for me. I acknowledge your presence but you are, as always, the unwelcome Christmas guest. So quite simply...

Fuck You Cancer!

Wishes for the Grieving

I wish you the freedom to grieve your way, and not let the untouched tell you how to do it.

I wish you the space to scream, shout, laugh, cry, sing and sob; don't let others silence you.

I wish you the time and space to grieve without the uncomfortable trying to move you on.

I wish you the voice to say their name forever, and the company of those who enjoy hearing it.

I would wish you my perspective without my pain, but I know that it's too late for that.

So remember your grief is love, love is good,
you are love and love lasts forever.

Princess Positivity

My grief has become like a comfortable blanket that I am wrapped in. Snuggled up and safe. I recognise it, it is mine and I don't ever want to lose it.

It's no longer a constant bed of nails, unbearably painful, a constant pricking of my skin so I can't focus or concentrate on anything else. The physical pain, originating in the centre of my chest, crushing and constricting, so tight that I am convinced I will die.

Those nails are now blunt, still there, making their presence known, but not piercing my skin like a dress of thorns. I can very quickly be taken right back to that crushing pain, as long, icy fingers tighten their grip on my heart and squeeze so hard it might implode. But it's not my constant place of residence anymore.

I, and others like me, are not allowed to live with our grief. Why does the World want us to get over it? Why is the expectation that sometime soon after the death of our loved ones we will simply stop grieving? The quicker the better, proving how strong we are.

Widows emerging phoenix-like from the flames, wiser, stronger, lessons learnt and, in my case, with a shiny new alter ego, "Princess Positivity", there for the World to see.

Grief is seen as something bad; a dangerous and incorrect response to someone you love leaving your life forever. Whereas actually grief is good. It's a normal, natural and healthy response to a devastating, obscene and torturous event, that you will never "get over".

We live in a death denying and grief adverse culture, where the absence of grief means we can all exist in a bubble believing we will not die. We will all live happily ever after, a modern day fairy-tale. With Princess Positivity as an everyday hero.

Reality check. There is no escaping death. As you read this you are now closer to your inevitable death than you were before you started reading. Princess Positivity says that knowledge should help us all live in the present moment enjoying our wonderfully precious time limited lives.

My grief has fuelled Princess Positivity, I love her and all that she represents. But I also love my warm, comfortable blanket of grief. I want to wrap myself in the pain, immerse myself in the memories, good and bad. Cry, scream, swear and shout. I'll tell Princess Positivity to fuck right off and allow myself to feel shit. Acknowledge that it hurts like hell. Be honest, that I wish it were different. Under that blanket I honour my feelings and accept my pain.

I know that grief is the price we pay for love and I wouldn't change that for the World.

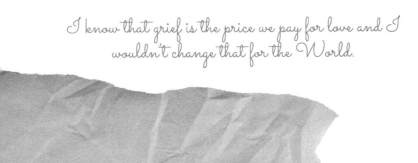

Grief Personified

Grief is angry. She glares at me and screams "What the fuck are you looking at?" I move towards her, eyes lowered, head bent, deferring to her power. "Fuck off", she screams. "I know you are going to try and make me feel better, I don't want to feel better, I like how I am feeling right now. I don't want your comfort, your soft soothing voice and your gentle arms. I want rage." She yells as she advances towards me. Eyes angry, nostrils flaring, pure hate in her eyes. She raises her arms, her hands clenched into fists as she begins.

I curl into a ball, as near to a foetal position as I can manage. Experience tells me it doesn't hurt quite so much if I am in this position. Her pounding is fast and furious as she uses her strength and power to beat me. Hard fists beating my soft flesh, again and again, no space in-between. Constant pain as one punch blends into the other. She is beating the living daylights out of me and I feel myself fading away. The pain, so consuming that I don't want it to stop. I want it to hurt so much, I want the pain to consume me, to engulf me, I want to become one with pain. I want pain. I am pain.

"No", she screams "You are not getting out of it that easily. Stay with me you bitch." Her punches begin to slow as her energy fades at the signs of my submission. Instead she starts to shake me. Grabbing me by my shoulders she shakes and shakes, my head flopping like a rag doll. Her screams are fading, changing into murmurs and sobs. I can't understand her mumbles but I recognise the sobs and I know what is coming next.

Grief is sad. Not that low mood, they didn't have the ice-cream I wanted, sad. It's the end of the world, I want to die kind of sad. She looks up at me with her big green moist eyes, so deep and wet you could drown in them. Her lip quivers and her voice begins to break as she whimpers 'It hurts'. She winces as she says it and you can see the pain. 'It hurts so much. I can't breathe. What is this pain? My chest. My heart. Oh god it hurts.' I move to her, arms open as I scoop her into my embrace. We gently rock as she cries an ocean, silent tears rolling down her cheeks, a waterfall of misery.

She accepts my kindness and care but it makes no difference. The sadness is so intense nothing can soothe

her. Deeper and deeper. Down she falls. A pit of despair, no light, no fresh air. A dark dank miserable existence, that's all she can see. 'This is my future. I have no future." She sobs. She starts to fade. I feel her giving up. I shake her as she had shaken me, although with less force. "No, stay you bitch," I murmur softly into her ear, my lips brushing her cheeks. Her eyelids flutter, I see fight in her eye, a laugh escapes her lips as she raises her head and straightens her crown.

Grief is strong. She is the Queen of Love. Only those who have truly loved and truly lost can live in her realm.

She is strong, she is brave, she is me.

The Final Sunset

In February he had been told he had days or weeks left to live.

In March he perked up a bit!

"I want to see one more sunset," he said.

He was bed bound. It wasn't going to be easy.

But team Martin wasn't going to be beat.

We hired a private ambulance from St John's. Two wonderful volunteers, who wouldn't take a penny in payment, transferred him from his bed at home to a stretcher, and the ambulance, with care and consideration, as if he were the most precious cargo.

We travelled down to the beach where we were met by family and friends.

We smiled, we laughed, we drank champagne.

We watched him, watching his, final sunset.

In June he died.

I never take a sunset for granted anymore.

Today

Today I am sad.

Today I am angry.

Today is not a good day.

My usual "enjoy the memories attitude" is not helping.

My usual "grief is the price we pay for love and I'm lucky to have experienced deep love" mantra is not enough to ease the pain.

My usual "he lives on in my head and my heart" belief feels like nonsense.

Today I will allow myself to be sad.

Today I will allow myself to be angry.

Today I will make the best of a bad day and live with my broken heart.

The night before the end

Right now, as I recall this time four years ago, I am filled with a strange sense of peace. That is unusual.

This time four years ago, I was experiencing a living hell whilst my darling man was experiencing a dying hell.

Nothing prepared me for that night and nothing usually comforts me when I recall that night. Yet tonight, I feel a strange sort of peace.

Martin had wanted to die at home with no strangers involved and as little medical intervention as possible. He got what he wanted and I don't regret it for a single moment.

There is a downside to that though. Often the medical profession protects us from some of the more graphic and upsetting sides of dying. Dying scenes in films and on TV are usually alluded to rather than shown and if they are shown it is some sanitised and romanticised version. Believe me there is nothing clean and romantic in what the girls and I came to call "death juice".

Usually I am focused on that – the gore, the guts, the pain, the trauma. It's as if I am reliving those awful moments and they are all I can remember.

Tonight, I am remembering more. I still have tears prickling my eyes as I recall sitting on the bed, holding his hand, telling him I loved him as he took his last breath. I still remember the crushing pain in my chest, like no pain

I have ever felt before or want to feel again, as I realised his next breath was not going to come.

But mostly I am remembering his smile, his twinkling eyes.

Mostly I am recalling his touch, his kindness, his calmness.

Maybe it's time that has made me feel this peace. Perhaps it's the candles and firelight I am bathed in as I sit in the very spot in which he died.

Maybe it's the after-effects of the vodka or the oxytocin from snuggling my granddaughter as I tucked her up in bed.

Who knows?

I am sure I will cry tomorrow, get angry and feel at war with the world.

But right now,
I feel peaceful.

And that is good.

Somethings are outside time…

In December 1992 Martin wrote those words, a poem, declaring his undying love for me; constant, unchanging and strong enough to stand the test of time.

In July 2019, I had those words tattooed upon my arm; ink in flesh, a bittersweet reminder of the love we had and how, in the end, time defeats us all. But as always he was right.

Somethings are outside time. His time may have ended but my love for him has not.

Love is outside of time.

Everyday

Not a day goes by when I don't think
of your name.

Not a day goes by when I don't
feel some pain.

Yet every day I live my life,
So thankful that I was your wife.

Every time I recall your face,
your smile, your touch,

I know that I have been lucky
to experience deep love.

No regrets, I embrace the pain,
And know that I would do it all again.

Grief and Guilt

When someone you love dies, you feel guilty.

Martin told me that. He had experienced the death of a wife and a child. He told me he was angry that no one warned him how guilty he would feel. How he would look for ways to blame himself – were the mushrooms he cooked for his daughter the night before she died not the freshest? Could old mushrooms cause meningitis? Crazy. He knew of course, that this was not the case but when deep grief has a hold of you, crazy thoughts emerge and you feel guilty, even when you are not.

We had this conversation early in our relationship and he said whenever he got the chance, he shared this insight with people. So that one day, when they might experience deep grief and guilt, they could at least be prepared and understand that beating themselves up, looking for ways to blame themselves, asking themselves what they could have done differently, was a normal part of the grieving process. That many people had experienced it before and it wasn't just them going crazy.

BROKEN

Twenty-three years later, I found myself in need of this advice. Martin died. Cunting cancer. I never knew such pain was possible, but I didn't feel guilty. I didn't look for blame. I didn't wonder what I could have done differently. It was cancer's fault he died, not mine. I couldn't have done anything different. I had given him the death he wanted, at home, with people he loved. He had a good death. Throughout our two year cancer journey we often used the mantra, "good life – good death – good grief".

Boy had he had a good life; we were trying to make sure he had a good death and this would hopefully ensure the girls and I experienced good grief. It wouldn't be easy, he warned us. It wouldn't be painless he said. But it would be the best that grief could be because we would know that he had a good life and we had done all we could to ensure he had a good death.

But then it hit me. Five months after he died the guilt demon got me. I felt guilty. And I wasn't sure there was any way back...

November has never been my favourite month, usually wet, usually windy, usually cold. November was Martin's birth month. November was nearly Christmas. And at some point during November 2015 it hit me.

I had been a widow since June. I had lived through the sadness and pain and had tried my hardest to stay positive and remember his life, not his death. In November that changed.

90

I developed an obsession with the 19th of the month. The date on which he died. I replayed over and over the last 48 hours of his life, which quite frankly were hell. I would not wish those 48 hours on my worst enemy.

The guilt that Martin had told me about had me well and truly in its grip. I replayed his pain and suffering of those 48 hours in my head, like a horror movie, and I felt guilty. I asked myself; *what could I have done differently? Why couldn't I have made it better? How could I have allowed the man I loved to go through those 48 hours.* I had failed to give him a good death. The motto "good life – good death – good grief" changed. It was now good life – bad death – bad grief. As much as I tried to be rational and talk myself round, I couldn't and my grief became all consuming. Goodbye Ms Positive Widow, Hello Ms Miserable Widow.

The slightest thing would trigger feelings of guilt, regret, sadness and failure. I had time off work, missed social events and was hard work for those who loved me. But they loved me, even though I was hard work.

And then I decided I couldn't go on like that. I had to give up or "woman-up". Despite my low self esteem and feelings of despair, I knew I couldn't give up so "woman-up" it was to be. I had three sessions of counselling with an amazing counsellor from Trinity Hospice and I found my way through it. I haven't been able to write yet about where the guilt came from and how I got through it. It will be painful to write and maybe uncomfortable to read. Maybe I will never be ready to write it.

I write for two reasons.

- The first is selfish. Remembering, and writing is like squeezing a spot – messy and uncomfortable at first but in the end you are glad you did it!
- The second reason is a bit arrogant, but I think if I can share a little bit of what I've been through with you, it might help you, it might help someone else.

It might help – just a little.

Guiding Star

He is my guiding light. He is dead, yet his life still guides me.

He taught me how to grieve, before he died.

When we met I suddenly believed in love at first sight. Those eyes. They twinkled and were kind, yet they were deep and sad. I couldn't work out how those eyes could be so twinkly yet so sad.

I soon learnt. His wife and daughter had died. He was living, yet not living. He was existing, yet not enjoying.

And then he loved me. Happiness shone in his eyes. We had two beautiful daughters. Joy radiated from his eyes when he looked at them.

But the sadness in his eyes lived alongside the happiness and joy.

The duality of grief.

He taught me love is possible after loss.

He taught me that you can be happy and sad.

He showed me it is possible to love the new whilst still loving the old.

I thought I understood.

He died.

And then I really understood.

Martin Walsh, my guiding star;
in life and in death.

All You Need is Love

One of my favourite memories of Martin was just before he died.

He lost all track of time and night and day blurred into one. About 4 o'clock one morning, when everyone but him and I were asleep, he started singing, "All you need is love, brup,brup,brara,braa, all you need is love,brup ,brup,brara braaa."

"Shhhhh" I said "It's 4 o'clock in the morning."

"Is it?" He asked.

"Yes, try and get some sleep," I pleaded.

He laid quiet for maybe five minutes. I started to doze in the chair next to the hospital bed that had become part of the furniture in our living room.

"All you need is love, brup, brup,brara,braa, all you need is love ,brup,brup,brara braaa."

Again I told him it was 4 am and he should go to sleep. This repeated about four times in the next 10 minutes. He must have heard the frustration and irritation in my voice as I said,

"Martin I've told you so many times now, it's the middle of the night and people are trying to sleep." Looking like a child who had been told off when they don't deserve it he said, "I'm sorry. I can't help it. My brain doesn't work anymore."

The tiredness left my body and I replied, "No. I'm sorry, if you want to sing, we shall sing".

So we did, together we sang. One by one we were joined by the rest of the household. And we had a proper sing-a-long party.

Precious memories, and it's true – all you need is love!!!

The End

It's hard to say where the terrible stage started. Was it when he lost his grasp on reality? Was it the first time he didn't recognise me? Was it when the abscess on his stomach went pop and we could see into his insides? I mean really see inside of him. Maybe it was when the death juice began oozing out of his mouth? Who knows? And does it really matter – aside from saying that the last couple of weeks were not great and the last few days were a living hell? For him, and all of us that loved him.

Most people had stopped coming to visit by then.

"It's too painful to see" said one.

"I can't watch this man I love die," said another.

We didn't have a choice; well, I guess we did. We could have said 'Enough, a hospice is needed now', but we didn't. We had given him so much of the death he wanted and we weren't going to let the gore and guts stop us fulfilling his final wish; to die at home with the people he loved.

Looking back, for me the start of that stage of his life, his death, came bizarrely with a Facebook post.

From Martin to my Facebook page on 6th June 2015 it simply said, 'Abralliatinr of Houma'.

Sent at 4.04 in the morning. The look of horror on his face as he tried to recall what he had been trying to tell me. A moment of lucidity in what was becoming a very confused mind.

"It's in my brain now darling, the cancer," he told me. "I can't tell what's real anymore, I'm sorry."

Apologetic and gentle, moving swiftly into humour we laughed as I told him the day before he had us sweeping imaginary (real to him) spiders and "black things" that were coming out of the wall.

It seemed to have happened in less than 48 hours. One day it was normal, cheery entertaining Martin, holding intelligent sane and interesting conversations, the next day there were spatterings of craziness throughout the day, until soon, more of his waking hours were filled with bizarre interactions.

Eventually, we worked out he became less distressed if we joined in with the hallucinations rather than tried to convince him of our reality, we joined him in his reality. I never worked out if it was from the cancer or the morphine; it didn't matter. Sometimes it was amusing, sometimes it was horrifying.

"Excuse me", he said, as I was leaning across the bed to try and give him a drink. "You're in my way. I'm dealing with a serious incident here"

I looked across to the other people in the room, his daughters and niece. Collectively, it seemed we didn't know whether to laugh or cry. He spoke to them, they were involved in the conversation, he was a police officer, which of course he had been before we met. From his hospital bed, in our living room, he was dealing with a serious incident. I was a stranger, in the way and preventing him from doing his job. Cross, and impatient he told me that if I didn't get out of his way I was going to be arrested. We all played along with it; gone were the days of trying to bring him back to reality. I left the room, got out of the way as I didn't want to be arrested. I went into the kitchen and wept.

He couldn't read anymore, he would turn on his Kindle, look at the screen and say it was broken, the words were all jumbled up. We would look, they were fine. The iPad was a constant source of frustration, after the bizarre posts and his inability to use it we would try and hide it away, to protect him and us from the distress it caused. We would then be in serious trouble as we were trying to steal it from him. "You can have it when I'm dead," he said.

After being the most sociable of beings he didn't want anyone other than his inner circle around him. If I needed the loo, for instance, he started to scream and shout for me, if I left the side of his bed, he became distressed. For the most part *Team Martin* had reduced to myself, Ella and Lottie in the inner sanctum of the room he was dying in. Other people were in the front room, it almost became the waiting room; waiting for him to die.

I'm sure that other people may remember this stage differently, but sleep deprived, broken hearted and physically exhausted this is how I remember it. Thankfully it didn't last that long and he became awake less and less. Although I hate to admit it, it was a mercy when he was asleep more than he was awake.

I mentioned death juice. I could avoid mentioning death juice but I don't think I should, not if this is to be an honest account. If you or someone you know is in a similar position you may experience death juice, I wish I had been warned. If you are very squeamish, you should skip the next paragraph.

Changing his colostomy bag, after he became bed bound and too weak to do it was second nature to us. We had got used to the tumour that had grown outside of his bottom, which we sprinkled with crushed antibiotics and wrapped in a seaweed dressing twice a day. We had got used to, and Lottie was even fascinated by, the hole in his stomach that we could peer into and see how much pus and gunk was in it, poking gauze swabs in or rolling him over to try and drain it. But nothing prepared us for death juice. It came suddenly. Initially he coughed and green liquid came out of his mouth. After a while it seemed to be there constantly, you could hear it in his chest, a death rattle, you could see it trickling, sometimes pouring out of his mouth. This means it's really near the end the nurses advised us, probably less than 24 hours they said.

But of course, this was Martin. Three days. Three days of what can only be described as torture. For those of us around him a living hell. For him, a dying hell. I don't know what the concoction of drugs going through the syringe driver were at this stage, but it didn't seem to be an exact science. Sometimes he was pain free, sometimes he seemed in agony. He was rarely awake. It was impossible to get him to eat. We tried to get water into him with a nifty device like a foam lollipop dipped in water that he could suck. When he had been conscious and less near to his death, he had even asked for it dipped in single malt whiskey – which of course we did – it wasn't like it was going to kill him! He sure sucked hungrily on that sponge! But in those last few days it was even impossible to get him to suck so he could have water, it was as if he had lost all ability to control his body.

Even in the midst of this terrible stage there was some humour. His mouth, lips and tongue had become dry and cracked and we couldn't get any moisture in. The usual lotions and potions didn't work on such a severely dehydrated and dying body. "Try KY jelly, it has no taste and will do the job" suggested a district nurse. Cue a hysterical discussion about which one of us was off to the shops to buy some lube! Of course, we got some. Willing to do anything to make him more comfortable, I gently spread it on his lips, easing my lubed finger into his mouth. He jerked his head back and his mouth formed into a grimace as if experiencing the most disgusting taste ever. We all tried a bit – God it was disgusting! The next time that nurse came we got her to taste some so that she never advised anyone else to do it again. We laughed. He couldn't join in but if he could have, I knew that he would find it hysterical that one of the last things he ever tasted was KY jelly. I tried to replace the taste with a single malt soaked foam lollipop and water but he was too weak to suck and swallow.

The evening of the third night of the terrible stage had arrived. It was one of our Marie Curie nights which meant a nurse stayed over and looked after him so we could get some sleep. I hadn't been to bed in three days, I was exhausted. Throughout the evening family had visited, we all knew he couldn't last much longer. As each one left, they kissed him and said goodbye. The unspoken knowledge that it would be the last time they saw him filled the room and tinged the goodbyes with deep sadness. But hey, this was Martin. He had turned months into years and days into months. He was cheating death big time, so maybe they would see him again in the morning.

The Marie Curie nurse was a wonderful man called Matty. Matty also worked for the Hospice at Home team so we had a really good relationship with him. Martin liked him, trusted him. He wasn't a stranger and there was mutual respect which was really important to Martin. Even though I thought it was really close to the end I knew I could trust Matty so Ella, Lottie and I decided to snatch some sleep.

The girls went up to bed. I went to the dining room, just the room next door and laid down on the sofa bed. I cried. I stared into the darkness. I got up a couple of times to check on him. I didn't sleep but lay in the dark, resting, trying to restore my broken and exhausted body ready for whatever the next stage may be.

Sometime, I'm guessing around 3:30am Matty came in and said "Claire I think you should come in. He's restless and his breathing is really changeable." I have a little guilt about what happened next, or to be more accurate what didn't happen next. I didn't ask Matty to go and wake the girls. Should I have? Would they have wanted to be there the moment their dad took his last death? Did I deny them their final moments with him? Guilt and grief are intrinsically linked. I can't change what I did. I went into the room, I sat on the bed with him a while, listening to that shallow, yet raspy breath. The rattling of the death juice playing a sad irregular tune on his chest. I waited a while then moved to the sofa and began chatting to Matty.

I don't remember the earlier content of the conversation, I know I spoke of our wonderful life together, I know I talked of my admiration for him and his sheer determination to die in a positive manner and to make the most of every moment. I told Matty "He used to say *'life is not a cricket score Claire, it's not about who gets the most runs, the biggest numbers. It's about the enjoyment, the pleasure of each and every moment. Life is not about quantity, it's about quality'*". My voice broke as I said "and this isn't quality, the rest has been, but this – this is not pleasure and enjoyment, this is not what he would want."

There was a noise, a moan maybe, a word maybe. I don't know but a noise and his breathing changed. It was as if he had heard me. I went over, sat on the bed, and held his hand.

His breaths became less frequent, silent gaps in between shallow breaths, as I held his hand and told him I loved him. "It's ok babe, you can die now. I know you don't want to, but you can. It's time, you're not having fun anymore." I whispered those words again, telling him again and again how much we all loved him and how he would never be forgotten. The gaps in between his breaths became longer. Until.

The next breath did not come, I was holding his hand, I was aware of Matty holding my hand. The pain in my chest was so intense, like nothing I have ever felt before. My chest constricting, feeling as if I couldn't breathe, couldn't talk. My face was wet. I didn't know I was crying but somehow silent tears were flooding out of my eyes, running down my face at an alarming rate. I managed to get out the words "That's it, he's dead, isn't he?" Matty nodded confirming the worst moment of my life. I stayed there holding his hand looking at him, staring, unable to take my eyes off him. His chest seemed to be rising and falling again. Was he breathing? Was he still cheating death? Dare, I hope? "Matty, is it my imagination or is he breathing again?" Matty squeezed my hand and said "No Claire, he's not breathing. It's your imagination, he really is gone." I'm not a big fan of the five stages of grief, but hey, looking back there was my denial. It lasted only seconds but it was there.

I looked at the time, 4:36am, and climbed the stairs to break my darling daughters' hearts.

Tears on My Keyboard

Tears on my keyboard, tears on my face,
Downwards they travel as if it's a race,
Rolling and falling they land on the keys,
As crippling grief, takes me to my knees.

I've been on my knees before, been flat on the ground,
My sobbing in darkness, the only sound.
That ripping sensation as my heart wants to take flight,
Emptiness, darkness, nothingness; the only sight.

No dreams of the future, no joy in the now,
I just want to join him, if I only knew how.
"Still here for a reason," a phrase I repeat.
Love is the reason, the truth bittersweet.

And so I write, note my thoughts and my feelings,
Maybe the words may bring me some healing,
Or maybe you, if my words strike a chord.
So, I write and I cry, tears on my keyboard.

You'll be fine

You'll be fine; you always are.
You are strong, I so admire you.
You're so brave, I couldn't do it.

Words of comfort.
Words of praise.
Words to support.

No.

Words to deny.
Words to quash.
Words to hide.

Let us not be ok.
Let us not have to be strong.
Let us be scared.
Let us cry.
Let us be sad.
Let us just be.

And maybe we might be alright.

Life with a broken heart

Oh, there you are, the man who broke my heart.
Yet still I love you. I miss you.
My heart is still broken.
It has sticking plasters, bandages and glue holding it together.
It still works. It still beats.
It still loves.
Loves you, loves me, loves others.
    And **maybe** most importantly, loves life.

Life with a broken heart.

A Different Sort of Funeral

I attended my first, and I hope last, online funeral thanks to cunting cancer and cunting Covid. The service was a beautiful tribute to a beautiful human. My Auntie Bernie. A wonderful aunt, a loving mum, a fun, fantastic and much-loved Nanny. A good friend to many.

We all die. I accept this. I write about it. I talk about it. I have a strong belief that, in talking about our love and our loss, we remember the lives of the special people who have died and that makes the grief a little easier.

But, of course, all my beliefs have come from my lived experience, and my lived experience is pre pandemic. Our new way of living includes a new way of dying, and, perhaps, a new way of grieving.

Never did I think I would be looking at a computer screen, watching loved ones, in masks, huddled together in family bubbles, saying goodbye to someone for whom we all share love, someone with whom we are all connected.

Never did I think I would reach out and touch the screen, caressing the tiny image of my mum as she walked towards the coffin to gently place a rose; unable to offer real comfort or exchange oxytocin, soothing our grief with love. Tears flowing down my face. Sobs echoing, disconnected in my dining room.

Never did I think our way of living would become so compromised by a virus, that we would be so unable to fulfil our traditions and comforts around death. Those rituals that help us grieve and are an essential part of a healthy grief.

The crying together, shared tears, healthy sobs and wails, connecting us, acknowledging our shared pain. The hugging, the stroking, the comfort of hands on arms, arms round shoulders, acknowledging that we can't make it better, but we want to.

The wake. That after-life party. Reminiscing, sharing stories, drinking, crying, laughing sometimes even singing. I look back at the *'Leaver's Party'* after the death of my

husband. We sang, never have I heard a better rendition of *'Let It Go'* in my life. He would have loved that.

Some of that was denied, today, by this poxy pandemic. It has taken so much and I hate it for that. But it can't take it all from us. It can't take love; we still have that. It can't take our connections, we may be physically distanced but we are still connected by the love, and the memories.

Oh my, the memories. I could write all night of the memories that I have of my Auntie Bernie, including my 18th birthday where she drank so much and didn't want to stop partying, she declared herself invisible! Not cancer, nor Covid can take our memories.

And sometime, in the not-too-distant future, we will get together. We will raise a glass; we will share those memories. We will laugh and we will sing. Some of us may get invisible.

But the love won't be invisible. The love will be seen, as clear as the light of day. Forever.

Me and My Grief

I'm a bit of a sceptic. I don't buy into models of grief that we are all expected to follow. A process which will eventually lead to closure. The idea that grief is linear and we should all move through a series of steps until we are fixed, does not sit well with me.

The experiences of many of us with lived experiences of grief are so varied and changeable that it is hard to imagine a model of grief that covers all. I especially struggle with those ideas that we 'get over it' or that grief is time limited.

Personally, I believe that I have grown around my grief. The pain hasn't reduced, I haven't moved on, my grief hasn't reached it's expiration date. It is still there, a huge raw knot of pain and turmoil, aching and longing, angst and love. But whereas it initially consumed the whole of me, every breath, every heartbeat causing pain, every thought, every moment engulfed by hurt, it can no longer consume the whole of me, because I am bigger, I have grown.

I didn't notice it at first, I didn't know that was what was happening. I never thought the pain was getting less. I never felt my grief was diminishing. At first, I thought it was that I was just getting used to it. Grief was the new pair of shoes, and I was wearing them in, so the blisters weren't quite as raw.

Overtime though, I noticed. I noticed that it was me that was changing, not the grief. Each day living with his absence changed me. Every moment wishing for his presence altered me. Each tear shed, every sob that escaped, made me a different person. Some people may shrink as they experience grief. I grew. Neither is right.

His determination, tenacity and drive to have a good death, became my determination, tenacity and drive to have a good life, with good grief.

As I became bigger and grew around my grief, it no longer consumed all of me, it no longer rubbed against me causing constant pain. Maybe that's what people mean when they say "it gets easier". It doesn't get easier because it goes away. It doesn't get easier because you get used to it. It gets easier because you grow and it no longer consumes all of you, because you are bigger than the grief.

Missing You

Your smile, your eyes, your taste, your charms.
Your smell, your laugh, the feel of your arms.
The way you insisted rolls were barms.
These are things I miss about you.

The hugs, the cuddles, the gentle strokes.
The tenderness your touch provokes.
Your awful, lousy, rubbish jokes.
These are things I miss about you.

Your personality, so immense.
Your political opinion, so intense.
The clothes you wore - no fashion sense.
These are things I miss about you.

The man you were, a real good guy.
The stereotypes you chose to defy.
Your lack of skills in DIY.
These are things I miss about you.

The good, the bad, the in-between.
The love we had, so extreme.
Proud to be on your team.
I simply miss you.

Things To Do on the Tough Days

There is plenty of advice out there on things to do to try and self soothe at the times where you want to feel a bit better. I stress the word want because if I'm honest sometimes I don't want to feel better. Sometimes I just want to be sad.

Sometimes I just want to honour the grief, to cry, to sob, to grieve. Society puts pressure on us to hide our grief, to bury it. People encourage us to feel better, or get over it, as visible grief makes them feel bad, it is uncomfortable. But sometimes we just have to acknowledge the pain and sit with our sadness, no matter how uncomfortable it makes the rest of the world.

However, on those days where I want to feel better, these are somethings that work for me:

- Music, loud and all consuming
- Dancing
- Getting together with good people
- Being creative
- Cooking (and eating!)
- A change of scenery
- Getting lost in a good book
- And of course, writing!

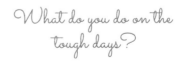

What do you do on the tough days?

I am changed

You are different, so they said.
You're not you, since he's dead.
Be the old you, they ask in vain.
We don't like to see your pain.

Time ticks on, it's over now.
Move on girl, do you know how?
You can't stay, stuck in grief.
Surely you want to feel relief?

My grief is permanent, a sign of my love.
Not something for you to be intolerant of.
Just let me be who I am,
A widow grieving for her man.

I am changed, yes, you're right,
Grief lives in me, like a burning light.

Meeting Him

It's really important when you are grieving to remember the good times. To remember the story of your person. To not let their story die with them. Here's the story of how I met him...

Twenty-two, a single-mum to a beautiful two-year-old girl. I was doing all right. Life was Okay. Living on benefits in a flat in South-East London might not be everyone's idea of Okay, but for me it was Okay. I wanted more though. I wanted to be a person my daughter could be proud of. I wanted to show her that working-class girls could have aspirations, good careers and achieve what they wanted.

I had worked in a nursery whilst doing my A-Levels, I had a toddler, I loved reading, I loved singing, I loved kids. My career choice was obvious – a primary school teacher, of course. But Uni, with a two-year old, how would that work? An article in a local paper told me that the Council was offering twenty free nursery places for single-parents returning to full-time education. Just twenty places on offer – but BINGO! I applied and got one of those free childcare places, applied to the local university and was offered a place on a Bachelor of Education degree, specialising in primary education. I was to be the first person in my family to go to university and I felt proud, and determined to make the most of my university experience.

Freshers' week; opportunities galore. The chance to join

a union, and I did. Before I knew it I was the union rep, for my course, which came with the chance to attend a training course, with the promise of free accommodation in a hotel and three meals a day. I'm not going to lie, as much as I was interested in politics, the draw was the food. I wasn't starving or wasting away by any stretch of the imagination but finances were incredibly tight and pasta, tuna, potatoes and eggs formed the main staples of our diet. I couldn't remember the last time I had eaten meat aside from very cheap minced beef.

Oh, how the other half live. The nerves and anxiety I had felt on the train, leaving London and my daughter, Bella, disappeared as I looked at the magnificent mansion in front of me. The taxi from the train station had driven me through the lovely Lincolnshire countryside, up a sweeping drive, lush grass, ducks, sheep and an obelisk as we drove towards what I can only describe as a palace. From Peckham to a palace, I thought to myself as I thanked the driver and made my way to the reception desk. Surely I was in the wrong place – this didn't look as though it had student accommodation, it didn't look as though it would have anything to do with a union.

I was wrong on both counts. The union owned the former stately home and ran it as a conference and training centre, choosing to host all of its own training events there as well as being open to the public. As such, the bedrooms in the main house were not for the likes of me. The student accommodation did exist, back up the drive, to an

accommodation block, a halls of residence type building leftover from the days when the building had been a teacher training establishment rather than a hotel.

I unpacked my bags, checked out the itinerary and traipsed back down the drive to that magnificent building, admiring the architecture. The turrets and towers glistening in the autumn sun.

Entering one of the training rooms on the first floor, I spied an empty chair and sat. A girl a similar age to me sat next to me and we began to chat and exchange pleasantries.

Briefly introducing themselves, the tutors set us our first task. "Reciprocal interviews. Find someone you don't know. Find out who they are and why they are here, then swap. After five minutes you will introduce them to the group and vice versa."

I still get butterflies in my stomach as I remember the next moment. I turned around and looked behind me, my eyes searching for someone interesting looking to introduce myself to. I may have had an ulterior motive, another hunger that I was hoping the weekend might satisfy. Anyone here who I might be able to have a one-night stand or weekend fling with I wondered. After all it wasn't always easy finding such opportunities as a single-parent!

A quick scan and no one caught my eye as a potential all night stand. However, I was curiously drawn to an older guy sat behind me. There was something about him. His eyes, all wrinkles and twinkles! His eyes were kind, cheeky, sad and soulful – all at the same time. I couldn't tell you what he was wearing, I couldn't tell you anything about him at that stage, all I could see were those beautiful, deep-blue inviting eyes.

His lips curled into a smile as I stood and walked towards him, dragging my chair behind me.

"Hi, I'm Martin," he said.

"Hi, I'm Claire."

He spoke first telling me of his late start in teaching, explaining he was in his 40s and had been a police officer for many years but fancied a change of career. A shadow passed over his face as he said this. Not the whole story, I thought, not my business though. He explained he was passionate about justice and fairness and that as a second-year student his peers had persuaded him to put himself forward as the union rep for the course.

"Not such a noble story from me I'm afraid," I told him. "For me it's the lure of three hot meals a day, and apparently there's a Jacuzzi," I grinned.

Time to introduce each other to the group. I did him justice, telling of his passion for fairness, his colleagues' faith in him to represent their views, painting the picture of a good man as my instincts told me. He grinned a cheeky smile I would come to know and love.

"This is Claire, she here because it's been a while since she's had any meat and apparently she's looking forward to meeting a man called Jack Oozi. I think it's his lucky day!"

I don't remember the rest of the afternoon, or indeed the rest of the course. But it must have been good as I have remained a life-long active trade unionist. In fact, even after leaving the profession in 2018, three years after Martin's death, I couldn't bring myself to leave the union, instead transferring my membership to the *left profession* status. What I do remember though, is realising less than 48 hours later on the train journey home that I had fallen in love with a man 22 years older than me who lived 200 miles away. How inconvenient.

We had eaten together on that first night and I discovered he didn't like pudding but still ordered one and gave it to me! Retiring to the bar after dinner we found ourselves in a group chatting but by the end of the evening, we were the only two in the bar and the bar staff were looking at their watches.

"Do you want to come back to my room for coffee?" he asked. Of course, I did.

We walked back up the drive towards the accommodation block, our fingers grazing each other's gently, surely just from the unsteady walk of two people with a few pints inside them? It couldn't be more, could it? Have you ever felt that uncertainty? Was there attraction between this most unlikely of couples, the northern older man, a widower, as he had revealed to me in the bar and a southern young single-parent? I had to know. Before we entered the accommodation block I reached out for his hand and held it firmly in mine as we entered his room.

"Tea or Coffee?" he asked.

"I don't drink either" I replied. He later told me that in that split second, he asked himself "What the hell is she here for then?", not believing that I could be interested in him romantically or sexually, but before he had chance to verbalise that thought I rendered him speechless by placing my lips on his and kissing him. Maybe I had found my one-night / all night stand after all.

People say you never forget your first kiss but I couldn't tell you about my first kiss, I can't remember it at all. But boy can I remember that kiss. By the end of it I knew that this would be no one-night stand. I was excited and terrified all at the same time. I did not want a relationship, especially not with a 44 year-old, ex policeman who wore jumpers!

I resolved there and then not to have sex with him (as it may have been my intention prior to the kiss!) fearing that if I felt such an overpowering feeling of attraction, connection and yearning after just one kiss, what on earth might I feel if I had an orgasm! Moving towards the bed we laid down and I said,

"I am not going to have sex with you".

His gentlemanly reply made me like him even more.

"I'm not expecting you to, but I would like to hold you in my arms and talk some more."

Our easy conversation continued whilst holding each other tight, stopping our chat momentarily for delightful kisses until we fell asleep, wrapped in each other's arms, fully clothed on a single bed.

November 14th 1992, forever imprinted in my mind as the first night I slept with the man I wanted to sleep with for the rest of my life.

As it turns out it was only for the rest of his life.

Little Things, Big Reminders,

Of course, there are the big things that bring your person straight to the front of your mind. The birthdays, the deathdays, the anniversaries. But there's so much more, isn't there? Some reminders are welcome, enjoyed and trigger-happy memories that remind us, although they are dead, they live in our heads and our hearts forever. Some reminders are not so welcome, taking us instantly back to a place of immense pain and all-consuming grief, where, no matter how long it has been, it feels just like it did at the start. They say grief is the price of love, so maybe we should even try and accept those ones, as they are a sign of love, but when it hurts that much, it's hard to feel grateful and as always, it's about what you feel. Not what they tell you to feel.

The little things. A song. This happens so much. Martin had a beautiful voice and played the guitar. 20 years of sing songs and his favourite songs, and all it takes is a particular song on the radio and I'm remembering. Singing along, twirling and dancing remembering the happy times, yet wishing for his voice, not that on the radio.

The little things. The colour orange. In an attempt to explain some mathematical concept to me he once said "It's like saying, the answer to the question do I love you is orange". And there it was, our new shared language. From that day on the word *Orange* meant I Love You, and still does.

The little things. A feather on the floor, many people believe in this as a sign. Martin didn't believe in an afterlife. And thought even if there was one he would be unlikely to end up with angels. Quote "and if there is an afterlife babe, I'll send you something much better than a feather!" I live near the coast and frequently see seagull feathers, they still remind me of him, his strong opinions and I often wonder what the, even better, would be!

The little things. A syringe. Not a happy one, and yet, it makes me smile. The chemo gave him a blood clot. He needed daily injections. I had been scared of needles all my life. I had to learn to inject him daily. The nurses taught me, they modelled saying at the point of entry 'a sharp scratch'. I changed it, as I pierced the needle into his skin I would say "Little Prick" Every day for six months I called him a little prick. When I see a needle now, I smile and think of him, my little prick.

The little things. A sunset. You may have read of his final sunset. I cannot see a sunset now without remembering. Remembering him, remembering his final sunset, remembering his life and his death.

Little things, big reminders.
Reminders of a man with a big personality and a huge capacity for love.

Things That make me go
Rrraaaarrrrrrr

Things that make me go Rrrrrraaaaarrrrrrr,
Things that make me go Raaarrr, Raaarrr, Raaarr.
The woman who knew him but didn't mention his name.
I'm sure she thought she was saving me pain,
But actually pretending he didn't exist,
Left me feeling so fucking pissed!

Outpourings of grief for people you don't know.
The contestants on that reality show,
The rich, the famous, the celebrity names,
As if pain and grief is just part of the games.

People judging me, for my grief.
They have no idea, it beggars belief.
You're over it too quick, oh you're taking so long.
It's catch 22, it so fucking Pete Tong.

The cost of funerals, what's that all about?
Social injustice, day in and day out.
The rich get the best, in life and in death.
We're not even equal after we take our last breath.

Grief competitions, who can cry the most?
My heart is most broken, my grief is foremost.
We don't all grieve the same, when will you learn?
My grief is mine, and not your concern.

The beast that is Cancer, makes me so mad.
It ravaged my man, my girls' precious dad.
I hate when you say, he lost his brave fight.
He was strong, smart and brave, no loser in sight!

Things that make me go
Rrrrrraaaarrrrrr

When is it Finished?

A wise woman asked me when my book about grief would be finished and what it would feel like.

I thought. I thought about that a lot.

I came to the decision that it is finished and yet it would never be finished. I will grieve for ever. I will be a widow forever. I could write about it forever.

Yet I want it published. I want people to read it. I need people to understand my perspective. I want to reach out to people who feel the pain. I want to say, your grief is yours, and yours alone, but you are not alone. Some of us are also stamped with a tattoo of grief and we should share our stories, tell our truths and not let grief be hidden from sight, isolating us and telling us to get over it.

So, if that's what I want, I must reach the end. I must say those words "It is finished". I think I am ready to face that and have realised I will write about this forever, because I will have grief forever, I will be a widow forever.

So I answer that wise woman.

My book is finished and it feels alright.

The End

Big Thanks

Wow. Where to start? I can not begin to tell you how thankful I am to the people who have helped throughout my life, especially this grief journey.

Family and friends

The people who have, loved and supported me, even on the days when I was not the best version of myself. I'm not going to name you as I am so blessed there are so many of you, I'm bound to forget someone!

My Men.

Martin Walsh, of course. Without him there would be no book. In my head and my heart forever. Some things are outside time.

Simon Jones, the man who came after. Without him there would be no book. His love, support and encouragement have kept me going. He put paid to my lonely old widowhood and has filled my life with love, laughter and kids! A mending and blending life certainly keeps us on our toes.

NHS

Thank you to all the wonderful NHS staff who did their best to ensure Martin had a good death at home, especially the District Nurses and Hospice at Home teams. You are heroes!

Book People

So many people, including those whose books and blogs I have read, have inspired and helped me get my thoughts, feelings and ideas into words on paper in the form of a book.

But I'll name a few:

Viv Ainslie: my publisher, fun frivolous and flipping amazing!

Kerry Burrow; illustrator. The Ernie to my Bert! Huge thanks buddy, you are so talented.

Lucy Sheffield; the magical writing coach. I have learnt so much from you. You are awesome. (IKR).

Sarah Lynas; the coaching Lioness. Thank you for asking THE question and for keeping me accountable and thoughtful.

And to all the determined women in MIB Preston, Blackpool and Fylde. You are inspirational and have helped me on my road from widow to writer.

Lightning Source UK Ltd.
Milton Keynes UK
UKHW020206280921
391265UK00007B/487